Presented to

_____

by

_____

on

_____

© 2002 Standard Publishing, Cincinnati, Ohio
A division of Standex International Corporation
All rights reserved
Sprout logo is a trademark of Standard Publishing.

Heritage Builders® is a registered trademark of Heritage Builders Association.
Focus on the Family® is a registered trademark of Focus on the Family.

Printed in Italy
Project editor: Jennifer Holder
Assistance with text: Jennifer Holder, Lise Caldwell
Design: Robert Glover, Kurt Tuffendsam

Scripture taken from the HOLY BIBLE, NEW INTERNATIONAL READER'S VERSION™.
Copyright © 1995, 1996, 1998 by International Bible Society. Used by permission of Zondervan
Publishing House. All rights reserved.

09 08 07 06 05 04 03 02   10 9 8 7 6 5 4 3 2 1

Library of Congress Cataloging-in-Publication Data

Stortz, Diane M.
  Jesus loves you : a rhyming rebus story / written by Diane Stortz ; illustrated by Len Ebert.
    p.cm.
  Summary: A simple poem with rebuses assures children that Jesus always loves them,
no matter where they are or what they are doing.
  ISBN 0-7847-1364-2
  1. Christian children--Prayer-books and devotions--English. 2. Love--Religious
aspects--Christianity--Juvenile poetry. 3. Jesus Christ--Juvenile poetry. 4. Children's
poetry, American. 5. Christian poetry, American. 6. Rebuses. [1. Prayer books and
devotions. 2. Love--Religious aspects--Christianity--Poetry. 3. Jesus Christ--Poetry. 4.
Christian life--Poetry. 5. American poetry. 6. Rebuses.] I. Ebert, Len, ill. II Title.

BV4870 .S78 2002
242'.62--dc21
                                                          2001049811

Jesus Lo♥es YoU

a READ-the-PICTURES book

written by *Diane Stortz*

illustrated by *Len Ebert*

Standard
PUBLISHING
CINCINNATI, OHIO

Yellow shining,

flying by,

Who's wearing a red shirt?

Thunder and  ,

in the sky . . .

How do you feel in a thunderstorm?

Whatever the weather,
This will be true:
Always, forever,

The heavens tell about the glory of God.
The skies show that his hands created them.
Psalm 19:1

 to the ,

Skip to the store,

Find the blue birds.

Fly in an ,

Drive to the  …

How many seashells can you count?

Wherever you're going,
This will be true:
Always, forever,

I will be with you everywhere you go.
Joshua 1:9

Working a  ,

Drawing a ⭐ ,

Which crayon is your favorite color?

Raking the  ,

Washing the  ...

Point to the sponge.

Whatever you're doing,
This will be true:
Always, forever,

The Lord is good. His faithful love continues forever.
Psalm 100:5

 and ,

Start the day right,

Point to the puppy.

Snuggle in  ,

And turn out the ...

Point to the teddy bear.

Daytime or nighttime,
This will be true:
Always, forever,

I will lie down and sleep in peace. Lord, you alone keep me safe.
Psalm 4:8

Whatever the weather,
Wherever you're going,

Whatever you're doing,
Daytime or nighttime,

No matter what happens,
This will be true:
Always, forever,

 ♥ u

Nothing at all can ever separate us from God's love because of what Christ Jesus our Lord has done.
Romans 8:39

Welcome to the Family!

Heritage Builders
Helping You Build a Family of Faith

We hope you've enjoyed this book. Heritage Builders was founded in 1995 by three fathers with a passion for the next generation. As a new ministry of Focus on the Family, Heritage Builders strives to equip, train, and motivate parents to become intentional about building a strong spiritual heritage.

It's quite a challenge for busy parents to find ways to build a spiritual foundation for their families—especially in a way they enjoy and understand. Through activities and participation, children can learn biblical truth in a way they can understand, enjoy—and *remember.*

Passing along a heritage of Christian faith to your family is a parent's highest calling. Heritage Builders' goal is to encourage and empower you in this great mission with practical resources and inspiring ideas that really work—and help your children develop a lasting love for God.

***

How To Reach Us

For more information, visit our Heritage Builders Web site! Log on to **www.heritagebuilders.com** to discover new resources, sample activities, and ideas to help you pass on a spiritual heritage. To request any of these resources, simply call Focus on the Family at 1-800-A-FAMILY (1-800-232-6459) or in Canada, call 1-800-661-9800. Or send your request to Focus on the Family, Colorado Springs, CO 80995. In Canada, write Focus on the Family, P.O. Box 9800, Stn. Terminal, Vancouver, B.C. V6B 4G3.

To learn more about Focus on the Family or to find out if there is an associate office in your country, please visit www.family.org.

We'd love to hear from you!